The Portrait Gallery Called Existence

“*The Portrait Gallery Called Existence* is a catalog of reading experiences as much as it is a masterfully rendered set of addresses—Neeli Cherkovski’s lifelong apprenticeship to poetry culminating in a wry, searching, reclaiming set of poems that adjust form subtly in relation to the poet’s experience of the work and person he’s circling back around through each pass. These poems are edged by hand and ear with a care categories such as biography and autobiography can’t catch, and their beauty—of which there is a great well—is bound up with a moving sharpness of utterance that stands profoundly against harm.”

—ANSELM BERRIGAN, author of *Don’t Forget to Love Me*

“During an era when poets were dangerous to know and destroyed their bodies pursuing their art, Neeli Cherkovski stayed observant. From first encounters to final conversations, *The Portrait Gallery Called Existence* revives voices of American literary consciousness: Ferlinghetti, Ginsberg, di Prima, Coleman, Kaufman. I was one of countless crazy teenagers who learned something foundational from these poets, and I’m glad to revisit them by way of Cherkovski’s insight. *Existence* offers a syllabus for autodidacts and misfit readers, traces the poet’s literary and family lineages, and redistricts America according to its artistic brilliance. Cherkovski reveals the life that poetry shapes for us—a life that’s not so evident these days. By simply holding this book you keep San Francisco from disappearing.”

—EVAN KENNEDY, author of *Metamorphoses*
(City Lights Spotlight Series No. 22)

“Neeli Cherkovski was a natural born poet. With every portal open to everything and each moment, he breathed poesy from the moment of his birth to his passing. For this last collection, as if to summarize his entire life, he curated a portraiture exhibition of his poetic, creative and biological ‘family’ including his own self-portrait. Here, we see his lineage and the vision ever so clearly.”

—YUKO OTOMO, author of *In Delacroix’s Garden*

The Portrait Gallery Called Existence

NEELI CHERKOVSKI

CITY LIGHTS BOOKS
SAN FRANCISCO

The Portrait Gallery Called Existence

Cover design by Jeff Mellin
Text design by Patrick Barber

Library of Congress Cataloging-in-Publication Data

Names: Cherkovski, Neeli, 1945–2024 author
Title: The portrait gallery called existence / Neeli Cherkovski.
Description: San Francisco, CA : City Lights Books, 2025.
Identifiers: LCCN 2025005426 (print) | LCCN 2025005427 (ebook) |
ISBN 9780872869370 paperback | ISBN 9780872869387 epub
Subjects: LCSH: Cherkovski, Neeli, 1945-2024—Friends and associates—Poetry |
Poets—Poetry | LCGFT: Biographical poetry
Classification: LCC PS3553.H3534 P64 2025 (print) | LCC PS3553.H3534
(ebook) | DDC 811/.54—dc23/eng/20250314
LC record available at https://lccn.loc.gov/2025005426
LC ebook record available at https://lccn.loc.gov/2025005427

City Lights Books are published at the City Lights Bookstore
261 Columbus Avenue, San Francisco, CA 94133
citylights.com

To Robert Sharrard
1953–2023

Table of Contents

The Portrait Gallery Called Existence

For the Poets

I

nothing spells disaster
as well as does emptiness
3 a.m., long talk with Susan
that was good, hoping
for a miracle
every word a sovereign note

these poems
continue dying
no matter, no rain for months,
immense forest fires,
wildlife dying

we have new cabinets
in the kitchen, the Saltillo tile

we ordered
a fine sliding door
facing the redwood deck

lions roar no more
pandas face extinction

what am I going to do
with the ghost of Paul Verlaine

looking for a free seat
in the crowded café?

2

it's easy being
busy with home improvement
and inevitable loss

poems pass, that grace
of Jack and Diane and Michael
and Lawrence and Amiri and
Ken and Whalen and Gregory oh
man many more, where are you
Danny Propper? Jack Micheline?
Rexroth bold, ambitious? Duncan
in a black cape on 24th Street?
ruth in beat haven? Joanne on
the phone?

Lamantia drops in
for a potion, somebody
out there please conjure forth
a forest of old-growth wood

Allen is at the café,
he wants to know why
wasn't I at the reading
the night before? may I
sleep with your boyfriend?

I love you, old spirit
it was always exciting
sitting at your side
you were the elder—

1963, Papa Hemingway . . .
when I'm in the car
with my mother, she's
humming a popular tune
whatever happened to
Edna St. Vincent Millay?
Hart Crane 32 years old
jumping overboard

"The emptiness doesn't leave"

it speaks at the memorial reading
just on account, one moment
then it snows or it seems to snow,

truly there is
not a snowflake inside
or out on the hillside
where we live
you'll find a night breeze
strong trees and the
mourning dove

bungled like a shaman in an ancestral dream

O If I Had Written "Howl"

portrait of ALLEN GINSBERG

I'd own an ashram
and invite the kids to gather
you wrote "Howl"
in a blast of energy
each line a feast

if I had written the poem
I'd have painted Los Angeles
as you did Manhattan

I'd have written stretches of
stucco and miles of palm trees
and the aura of the freeway system

you played with your city
as if it were a trombone
you fenced around the
brooding skyscrapers

you wrote it and now you
have to live with it
and I will think sweetly of
the last time I saw you
in a photo gallery
your terrific
photos of the Beat
Generation

when we met you said, "You're fat"
I said, "You're bald"
the next day you told Ferlinghetti
I was angry because you wouldn't sleep
with me, the truth is
I had a handsome young lover
less than 60 feet away
on Bob Kaufman Alley

thank you for the poem, Allen,
for Kaddish and the Green Automobile
we miss you
we love you
we pick rose petals
                    off your tongue

On the Phone with Ferlinghetti

portrait of LAWRENCE FERLINGHETTI

at age 99
Lawrence phoned
to talk
about our last rendezvous
on the battleground of
Normandy

hey Neeli
why are you in New
Orleans? I said they
flew me first class
in a flying fortress
over the ruins of
Nagasaki

did you really like
A Coney Island of
the Mind?

yes, I was
13, that book and
Bertrand Russell's
Why I Am Not a
Christian carried me
through

“you should be poet
laureate,” he said, I
am already, I told
him, but nobody
knows it, they
don’t know how
I escaped from
the death camp
and landed in
the madhouse

and sipped
cappuccino in
Caffè Trieste
with poets
of the plain

today I’m
just an old
man with a heart
of bronze

dear Lawrence,
I buried you
in the poetry
room of City Lights
next to Allen
Ginsberg as
the minotaurs
saddled up
beside your
body laid out
like a rose

I praise
the shallows
of our Bay
and hope for
mercy as
a lantern at
night, truckling
Japanese moon and
Parisian amber

you wanted
to sail forever
into the wise and wild
stream

oh, I read
your Fearful Words
for Fidel Castro
beginning with a
quiet life in
Mike's Place

I am fortunate
for your good wishes
and friendship
in this three-act play

it was Aggie who said
call Lawrence
he wants to
talk to you
one more time

in the Whitman-like
intersection
where unspeakable angels
brace for the
darker decades
yet to come

I Am Starving for Silence

portrait of JOHN WIENERS

he was troubled by wisdom
whistling out of stucco
and cracked paint
God fills him with nail polish
and an ear for phantom lovers
on narrow streets of Boston
where he crossed the schoolyard
to find precious stone

tomorrow John is in love
he wants to pigeonhole humanity
while standing on a dime
we who love him do not wait
for his love, we who were children
grow judicious as mist
called old age settles

you see John came to town
on the back of a lion
who sang like a mourning dove

John wrote of memory
love evokes, he instructed
young men and women
to gather and to listen

John arrived in a small volume
of dynamite gently posited,
it was the age of Geiger counters
and lunch counter sit-ins
1950s Americana

I was 14 when his hotel room verse
broke my eyes . . .
he bumped into himself
and died in squalor
nailing fathers to the shallows

he picked up many things
from the brick oven
giving them language
you carry as if it were gold

you must know a few things
and hold them carefully
cautiously, don't trust anyone
over 200 years of age,
write joyous praise
of youth, "For in this country
it is terror . . ."

Irish eyes
ragged clothing
God knows he tried
skinny little room
on Beacon Hill
he said, "Oh, Mr. Cherkovski,
thank you for your poems. . ."

I thought he might be
a citizen of Rome
in the days of Catullus
Boulevardier
of that ancient citadel

goofy eyes, beautiful lips,
soft-spoken, how do you do?

Rimbaud for the First Time, 1957

portrait of ARTHUR RIMBAUD

I picked up the sweet
Peter Pauper Press book
with a drawing on the cover
of a kid with messed-up hair
and paid at the counter
then walked onto E Street
to Annabelle's Drugstore

ordered an ice cream soda
and read the poems, not even aware
they were from the French

yeah,
these poems seem to say, "rinse behind
your ears"

the way you clean me up
and slam me
into a blackboard

I read until sunset, then caught a bus
to the north end

rivers ran
through my head

you leave me falsehoods,
find madmen who could save us
from belief and false values

Rimbaud gave me the big
unwritten lines

Meeting Jack Micheline

1967 I drove on Melrose and turned onto Gower
made a wrong turn, hit Sunset
where I took a right to the old central core

nimble, quick, I am
thinking Mayakovsky
loved expansive human caprice
Jack romanticized him
I'd find out later

I parked on a dilapidated
block, Hamilton
Court, a truly drab facade
or it could've been
Kingsblood Hotel
or maybe there was no name
just an address

I buzzed 3A and gained
entrance, then climbed
three steep flights,
the air smelled of
cockroach spray, so much for
L.A. glitz

I knocked "Yeah! Yeah!"
a voice called out, moon-

faced man with Bob Mitchum
lips and delicate hands, stood
before me, I handed him a copy of
his first book, River of Red Wine

"I hope you're not a poet"
he said, sauntering to the edge
of an unkempt bed
and gesturing toward a chair

"I hide from poets. I prefer
madmen and criminals. The Poets
I like are outlaws, Rimbaud,
Villon, the Russians,"
he waved his arms over a ray of light
from flashing neon
streaming through the window

"What I'm saying is
I hope you didn't bring your poems."

"Bukowski sent me"

"Okay, he's alright"

"I read your work in some of the anthologies
'Streetcall New Orleans' and those lines, 'the people
are so nervous'"

"Never mind . . . never mind
I'll sign the book"

he reminded me of Sherwood Anderson and
James T. Farrell, rough American
wordsmiths, no theory, just words
dropped like iron piping
onto freight train flatbed

we went to the racetrack
the following afternoon

Quasimodo in the 3rd brought us down
we left in glum silence
back to town

53 years now, Jack long gone,
Bukowski under stone
I am an elder
who hobbles as he walks

Mayakovsky is a silhouette
the outlaws, o
those outlaws
"blue moon, blue moon"

Holy Ghost

portrait of WANDA COLEMAN

you came from South Central
Wanda Coleman, yes, you
and I were so young, you said
"who is the holy ghost?" well
now the world
is fifty years older,
we all knew you had the river
in the center of your art, yep,
i was a student of
astro-poetics, you studied
with Big John Thomas
and Bukowski, then you
took a class from Clayton
Eshelman, all these white guys
who were silver bullets

I never quite knew
what happened, who is
the father, how does the
daughter fare? what road
to an iron cross (ha!) you
even wrote a poem for
me and phoned to say
"Neeli, you were so
young in the shadows
of those mastodons
who roamed East

Hollywood just before
the lynching of JFK"

all those plaudits
you earned, all that
Blackness, all that
you wrote to set
the record straight,
your American Sonnets
seemed so rock-bottom
American, then you were
sick and died, you leapt
off the stage when
you read with Allen Ginsberg
and hugged me, heavy blue
woman as blue as the
blue heron, yep, Hank and
John still alive then, what?
1987 or?

"you remember me?"
you said, "hey, I remember
the holy ghost, I always
thought you were
that one"

Wanda,
wild thinker, so hard
you worked, all those awards,
all those books,
all that time, I
read you now
in difficult

days, your new selected
in the name
of the father
and his daughter
from the splendid
sprawling ghetto, L.A.

For Bob Kaufman, Poet

I said Bob you walked into
the kitchen
just in time, there were irises
on the terrace and women
with parasols
dreaming of dolls
smashed on the rocks
at the end of the road

I said there are elegant waiters
in Chinatown who will serve tea
in time for our lemons
to ripen, an old Catalan comes in
to order chow mein
he wears a black beret and paints
the California missions

life is stern
your idea is a drawing
fine lines
hint of reception
anger in truth
shallow ponds by roadside
I said Bob
this is my letter
I send it by regular mail

you rolled a cigarette
and struck a match
the room felt so small
dim lit kitchen, flimsy table,
I'm drinking coffee
you blow smoke onto a horn
that resonates everywhere
no wonder you tap a finger
on the table

Bob I'd like to say
you've drawn a line
the irises are handsome
they stand against time
no one can paint them
as well as they can
you see this and smile

when the Dante Hotel burned
you came to stay with me
and the black princess
of New Orleans, you were
uncompromising
through cold nights
we read aloud
from treacherous books
and through memory

music then is failing
to connect the dots, feeling
flees, sound bleeds
all over form, and you can

forget content
you know what I mean

the muse loves to dance
on old recordings, do flow,
so slow, cast a net, feed
the animals, rapid fire,
boom! bang! more we dare not
ask, piece a poet
out of bone, write in stone
come home
to your ashes spread
on a sallow day

forgive you I will
as I must honor the bleak
necessities and read the words
of Lorca and touch
those keys on Monk's piano
such spirit is endless

we were enlightened
by sentences that grew out
of our sea voyages, we saw
hart crane go overboard,
we waited at the bottom
of the sea for mermaids
dressed in silk, we drank whisky
at Li Po in Chinatown
down a gated highway
of the phosphorescent moon

The Elder Poet, Philip Lamantia

with Eric Walker

down from idle talk I walk
to where mystic rivers meet

eyes beheld wild eyed trees
on pasts further inside

Kora and her retinue
holding dangerous beads

pharoah runs to greet a barge
filled with words from desert deities

oh empty words
this earth is beloved

no other land exists
as far as a mime can see

make that poem out of silence
and spin it till solitude bleeds

take Delacroix yellow in tow
as timer tilts, thoughts glow

tell the poet *Lamantia* to light
another cigarette over the rain

meet him at Caffe Trieste
with wild young lion in tow

Eric sounds sweet but he angers
easily, there is no time he explains

where the path is steep we step
Lamantia rails, he pushes Rimbaud

grass turns sultry, sunlight dims,
coffee tastes bitter, Cuban sleeps

Eric wide-eyed, his grandfather lives
in a redwood tree on the smiling coast

LAMANTIA offers nothing less, everything
turns into a poem Eric wishes to know

STOP LISTENING, turn somber reverie
over a perfect moment

from jukebox Giuseppe Verdi
filters table to table, the path is sacred

move along gather rosebuds from
the queen, leave Eric to inscribe

do you hear LAMANTIA? he calls
from a floating garden: "DO YOU HEAR ME?"

as a kid of fourteen Philip embroidered
onto plain air, caught wild ponies

now as elder poet had time, he held
time, he saw mantle of demonic light

the real poem is you, words alone
don't describe, Eric was alive, 18

LAMANTIA remains now as he was
cigarette half ash, coffee gone cold

Elegy to Gregory Corso, Poet

greetings, mister,
you were a prince of poesy
now you are a book of piety
and honesty, we find it hard
to accept the pain
you introduce, so ruthless

brother bards
come into your words
and anoint the rush of
old age and death

step lively still
like a Celtic hipster
rousing, you seem
to circle Dante, how
vain you were, how
trapped in orphanhood,
celebrated for
the picture-perfect
"Marriage"—the all-too truthful
"Bomb"—you saw that
fat-assed authoritarian
angered, poised to strike

Gregorio, Gregor, death
loves us all, young Mozart

and old Whitman, seamstress
and Piccolo Pete, we die
in the cold or under
warm sheets, make for light
a deadly life, peace-loving,
neat, swift-flyers, of
song we never tire

tune-in, there is more
to come, a Golden Dot
with silver lining

That Poet

portrait of GIL OTT

the form glows as gratitude grows
our eyes meet in mythical North Beach
may I buy you a cappuccino?
forgive my inappropriate behavior
I love the dark lady who lived in my body
and caused grief
I fell for a young blond who resembled you
I learned my lesson walking on the embarcadero
you were baking a cake to try and get a job
all I did was laugh and dismiss
those touching lyrical poems flowing
knowing the true gold
is not to be purchased
not to be bought or sold
ask Vincent van Gogh

Gil, you died too young
there were awards in your name
I hear you on the internet
young man I knew
life says hold up your hands
you declaim life is sacred
your thin blond self
clatter of coffee cups
careful script, time rules

we follow the moon
to the dim courtyard
leaves scattered from ash trees
I did not know until too late
you chanted like
Homer, melody grows
on lemon trees—you may come
to sit on my deck and listen for crows

Where I Walk in Ecstasy

portrait of RUTH WEISS

one dark horn on the terrace
93 years torn into night
old world child forever modern
jazz woman
take a moment
tear a sheet of sky,
music broods
goes into a tunnel,
walls cave in, doom splits
us in half, mine the music

the sound of a piano
thrust in the side of a lantern
far enough away to be dangerous

when do we learn to leave the
simple bebop? why is that horn moving
like a bullet? mind the muse
of each note

walk ecstatic
where rhododendrons whisper,
they are one trail, these tallest trees
surrounding them are another,
your hand in mine, how
do you die? why are you
leaving so soon?

do you not recall
innumerable choices?
the sacred catastrophes
and profane pleasures
that make a poem?

Renaissance

portrait of HARRY SMITH

for Mahogany I would . . .

I would go to the woodshed
with a box of pastels
and sing till the man
ambled along
shoving abstractions
explaining truth
as four-edged sword

speaking of blue jays
I'd sprinkle glass
on the day of your
wedding and score
a kilo of historical notes
to enjoy summer's
garbage barge leaving
for the open sea

God grant hubris
to great gated city of cruelty
and perversion

Harry:
anthropologist
filmmaker

archivist
minster of song

grip the legendary heroic
meta-man, be like the serpent
in the chambers
where creation is elation

Harry dumpy dreamers
scrape clouds

Mister Golem a mystery novel
to those of us who wait

you kept a dead canary
on a bed of ice cubes
over the stones of Manhattan
into the smirking adolescence
of Arthur Rimbaud
before he was a coffee merchant
in the time of assassins

did you ever write a poem?
I know you lived inside of poems
insight was your technique
quietly centered
I'll not forget you were in a café
reading "A Season in Hell"

then they moved you into editorial
and stay you did for several centuries
a present
ran with a group of surrealists

poets and writers
trading lullabies and Gothic fantasies

I hold in hand a gift you gave
on my birthday
stories by Oscar Wilde
a handwritten aside
which I will cherish
until the last note is played

San Francisco Poet

portrait of A.D. WINANS

the man who drove
down the coastline
of his poems
he is 86
and not going anywhere
other than to the window
where he watches a leaf
on the street
barely avoiding
traffic as it is whisked
along by the wind

the poet speaks
for San Francisco
and of love affairs
and literary politics and
self-doubt and work
schedules and daily
walks and military service
Bob Kaufman and wide rivers

old Al
endurable
irascible
A.D. Winans
a slender leaf
driven by the wind

The Man from Paradox

portrait of SCOTT BIRD

few remaining condors
clutch versions of the sky

so beautiful a polis
we create when syncing
into sleep, lush gardens
and stone fountains,
we awaken in the town called Paradox
our idea is to follow
a bardic drummer-boy
and feel as if they had written us
into their poems

I love your Rocky Mountains
not unlike Brokeback Mountain
in desert places, sage coyote and bear
beaver and deer and muskrat

I love you as if you were my son
and there I lie
smiling

Animals
portrait of JOANNE KYGER

yes, you will never outrun
the gazelle in moonlight
or that bighorn on the high corner
nor will you stab
the lion in her heart
before you die of a fever

and no, never again, antelope
and wild stallion, sheep dog
in a mounting blaze, animals, God,
man, and his animals, man and
rats and poison trees, caged
nobility, freedom caged, whale as
entertainment, animals in a
lab, go feed the amorous light

yes, maybe, incredulous rift of
hot light, forest burning tight
late in screaming words of night
tiger louder, slender and
powerful, dog at your side, cat
on the doorstep, improbable
rim of silver dust, it's snowing
fire in a rodent tail, go blast out
one sustaining note
for every animal of our realm

Angel on Paper Noon

portrait of DAVID MELTZER

did you understand
silence in all poems?
do you ever traipse
the boulevard
thinking "I am guilty
of the other man's
conclusions?"

did he say "hello"
mid-morning crows
flying overhead?

**

centuries ago
we browsed the shelves
of a bookstore
down from the school
where we taught

I watched
as so many words
paced the pages
hungry and Dionysian

am I guilty
of an unknown rhyme

I was given your red notebook
and heard a song for delirious birds

you wrote a grandmother poem
which remained hidden
I was advised to love that old lady
and rip my own grandmother
from the pond
telling you she died
on a streetcar

I learn to listen
in a new way

For the Poet Diane di Prima

one afternoon it's a beautiful planet
is everybody sleeping?
stay well
old age is dying
late at night in somber tones

deer wander
a fox disappears
no, we don't need flowers
here in the Alps
only her harmonium

tell me, Diane, because I am thinking
all the way over to your room
in the care facility
I envision a photo
from the 1950s you perched
on a piano top
Swarthmore dropout

how you loved John Keats
those great letters
his negative capability
your floating bear
your love for younger
poets taken by Revolutionary
Letters, oh Diane

your devotion to “The Return”
“Exile’s Letter” and “The Ballad of
the Goodly Fere” all from
Old Ez, you visited him
in the madhouse
you and the ABCs of Reading
you and 1950s America
hello, LeRoi

so much depends on
what we seem
and where we stand

thank you for the clarity
and concision
larger than politics
you and Shepherd
here to read on
an elegiac night

Diane who rode
a dancing star

down the road
wise silence, the nurses
asked who is she
so many visitors
she keeps a schedule
at bedside, books
on either side
of bed

buses sneeze
on Mission Street
trees gossip
out in the fog
I smell medicines
an orderly with
crooked teeth

oh look, Diane
the sun believes indeed
after one hour we leave
forever blessed

invisible light

For Michael McClure, 1932–2020

you kept bringing logs to the fireplace
on that long-ago night in the Haight
I watched blue tongues of fire reach
your wall, "Don't worry," you said

and read a poem. you had been talking
biology to a scientist, a year earlier
I sat in your living room as you and
Allen Ginsberg spoke of taxes and write-

offs, no fire then, it was summer, but
we were now in mid-winter, the conversation
turned to the poetry of D.H. Lawrence,
you loved the animal poems "The Red Wolf,"

"She-Goat," "Elephant," then you recited from
memory, "And I think in this empty world there
was room for me and a mountain lion." Ha! I
thought of "Jaguar Skies" and your lines, "Let

me hug you, let me kiss you with my fingers
made of fame . . ." You wrote of cosmic molecules
our biological patriotism, I know you understood
Lawrence as a hunter of words; you sent

a manuscript, Simple Eyes, one day, there, you
were a child in the Midwest, young and
labyrinthine, geographer, oceanographer, student
of poesy, astronaut like you called Larry Eigner

when we buried him, so you come and go, old
men grow old, old poets grow ancient, the fire
rages, it burns the fields and terraces, and
sends bullocks into a frenzy, and turns to ash

My Friend Lawrence Ferlinghetti (1919–2021)

Ferlinghetti and I
would go to the Surf Theater
way out by Yokohama
he was an aggressive
driver, his old Volkswagen
had several dents

driving through the Stockton
Tunnel he'd proclaim,
"we're leaving the Casbah."
and he would chuckle
as he turned left on Van Ness
leaving North Beach
and City Lights Books

we saw a movie set in Paris,
the title escapes me, but
Lawrence's excitement
over the sights, Notre-Dame
in a side view, the Seine
head-on, Apollinaire's shadow
on Boulevard St. Germain

"I should go for a visit," he said,
"Like Henry Miller did."

two days later we headed
to Bixby Canyon, he said
I could carve my name on
the outhouse wall alongside
Kerouac and Ginsberg

we read from Leaves
of Grass that night by
a campfire, "he's like
an older brother,"
Lawrence said of Whitman

a year later
he wrote from
Paris, "I'm bringing you
a new beret, made right
here."

San Francisco, Paris,
Big Sur, an open
heart who would
never grow old,
who would be an
ancient bard, who
would hold a lantern
in the dark

he wrote
"The dog
trots freely
in the street"
and told anyone

who would listen
the secret meaning
of Goya's greatest scenes

February 24, 2021

Surrealnik

portrait of TED JOANS

do you stray from Indiana
to New York City 1950s
Theodore young jazz poet
Beat Generation
Greenwich Village parties
Avec les poètes
legendary in the days
of existentialism
Mr. Joans, not LeRoi Jones
or is it the other way around
black daughter realism
skirting icc
beloved comrade awake
father of many children
lively as loving can proceed
and that is the way
we fold our eyes
we passed through doors
revolving doors
meet you at the café
we will drink cappuccino
later meeting the poets
Ferlinghetti Hirschman
and Lamantia
in a basement
off Broadway
joined by André Breton

and Langston Hughes
other heathen royalty
we trade poems
share our strategies
sizable hands
saw the night lights
girlie joints, wise Surrealism
may we raise a banner
in the circle of survival
beatitude, you said, negritude
TIMBUKTU
hobo tithes
we have no other thought
than to rise
and be counted

I Praise the Splendid Goats

portrait of NANOS VALAORITIS

when they go trotting
after the moon, I love their
scraggy beards trimmed by wind

hey, Nanos, I used to visit your class
and write in my head about
the shape of red skies
as you brought Homer down to earth

I grew to adore those goats
troubling to rise above traffic
when you drive me home from
one place to another, imagine
those goats laughing at our foibles

the last time I saw you was
at your mother's
apartment in Kolonaki
when you were waiting to
have your television repaired

the repairman genuflected

the Bancroft librarians
soon cross the Bay
on white-maned Arabians
for the second installment

imagine herding goats up
Mt. Lycabettus,
you are in your late nineties,
daughter Katerina paints
and has commissions, sure
of herself
the goats wear chimes, hear
them, insatiable four-legged

I Think

portrait of JACK AARON HIRSCHMAN

I think what happened is
that I lost my bearings
dreaming of an ultimate poem
made of flesh and blood
I think what happened
is that this poem snuck up on me
while I was watering the plants
in my garden
I think what happened
is that my old poet friend
lit a fire way up high
in the benighted stars, sure
I suppose there are dancing lions
who carry hand-carved shields
and unicorns smiling
at greens of wheat and fields
of alfalfa, I believe, I swear,
I think what happened
is that the Red Sea parted
and the children passed
one by one into the channel
sure, my friend translated
a Yiddish poet from the holocaust
and thought it was a river
for us to cross, he dipped
his poem in the stream
and dreamed of carnage

I think what happened is
my friend wore a slanted hat
into the café way back then
when we were sleeping
on the Cyrillic beds, sure
I have an idea of what happened
when my friend crossed over
it's the mountains inviting him
in, the wild goats, it's a herd
of sheep, a ship of wine,
jars of honey on the wagon
passing our orchards, yes
I think what happened is
memories dropped out of
hey son, yes I do remember
my friend reading Russian
under the lamp, and aria
from Giuseppe Verdi
played out on the jukebox
oh come comrades demand
another dance, sure I know
what happens, what happens

I think the wild goats stare
before they nibble the grass
under twitching light, I feel
the power inherent in the poetic
mind, sure, then the new year
arrived, sing of the black bird
and seeing for the railroad
and talk the old acquaintances
into returning, yeah! why not
be so real? I think I know what

happened down the path
my friend the poet trekked
left bold tracks, I think
what happened is that you
are not slaves, he is not a machine
and this is only a dream
a fire, fortitude, and beatitude

August 27, 2021

Etel Adnan at 96

poverty grips
the canyon
and roots out
all we see

it's not exactly
heaven here
or a silent
wadi filled

with shards
of ceramic
vases, nor
does it look

like hell, must
be middle
ground, the
poet pains

the painter
animates every
room, we sat
at her side

in the loud and
crowded bar,
what do you
say? did you

paint a simple
sound? we were
at our table,
here, from Marin

across the Bay,
Etel, Simone,
Jack, Aggie,
all of us

at our table
might as well
have been
in Beirut or

Paris or on
drifting dunes
across apocalypse
and into tranquil

tracks leading
to other cafés
where she will
speak from far

distant realms,
I was lucky to
talk to her, to
surprise death-

defying darkness
down the hall
from the masters
of creation

For Mosab Abu Toba

He would suggest
staying clear
walking along the shore
like a child of god
believing in cornstalks
date palms
providing fruit
and shade from the heat
of the day

he would suggest
you stay safe
in this zoological park
we call the Earth
try to raise bees
and harvest honey
for an amber dawn to break

some of us are plagued
by crows and bluebirds
but you must survive
in a world of drones and
shrapnel
no wonder your poems
are planted

by the desolate sea
and breathe
acrid smoke

I think of Ibn
Arabi like an oasis
in the wasted caliphate of
fear, and one day will
bring you to my garden
to break bread
drink a cup of wine
and sound out
the beauty
of a red rose
growing in the ruins

February 8, 2024

She Talks Oblivion
portrait of ANNE WALDMAN

quiet as a roaring furnace
the full moon is out

be purified in speed

last slinking fast moving
breathing single units
of probability

only seconds to go

taller than grim home-town
the gaze firm and focused
trekking
where Bashō
once trod famously

think of Bodenheim and Millay
and cummings and Allen Ginsberg
crowded into a corner
of Bohemia

where I am a nudist
Buddhist alive

Anne's poem "Cabin"
needs proceed

over precarious summer
ignoring the void

        young we are ever
    a month or so
above and beyond
Nagasaki burnt into a rock
            assigned to grass

who is a sister in the shelter
of the cabin?

        if you are believable
and loud
I wait for the sound of poesy to congregate
on a storm-lashed bluff

        colored ghost
in all possible retrievals
the ark for empathy and creation
what would a man be alone in the cave?
ask any poet-saint
how do I build an abode
tonight when a cool breeze
scatters light off an aspen tree?

"A Cabin in the Clearing"
or the labyrinth
in which her voices preside

* * *

on the corner from New Jersey
and New York and Boulder, from secret
peaks north of Portola
from ethereal mist
from fast-trekking mind
to mindless song
from the way she stands
on a stage reeling
out, from light she
talks oblivion, from
rebirth to equinox
not for a moment
will she not step
forever, every sound
a habitation, her palms
never close, do not glow
alone, grow solid
in one performing
circle, let it
rain, we hold truth
inevitable, tall, lovely
lace, flowing blooms, white
tiger drawn through
ancient pause, it rains
on the streets of
NY, see the
wet concrete

here the poet
saw and read
into every confusion

Song
portrait of BOB DYLAN

is Bob Dylan a forest
or a tree? will he come to the
meadow and play a song for you and me?

Bob built a sprawling house in the Malibu hills
it has double doors and well-made windowsills

he travels the world in a private plane
sings wild wisdom
against public grain

he stayed sane and did his part
for more than 60 years
he dabbled at his art

does he not love the animals?
boarding Noah's ark?
his guitar is a piano,
a tambourine at heart

he performs in music halls
on a blue cloud
where Father Whitman
smiles from his shroud

Bob comes from Hibbing
way up north
a man of humble origins
he traveled to New York

do you not see him performing
like the musical lark?
trust his soul, he will not
abandon you in the dark

Safe in Heaven Dead

portrait of JACK KEROUAC

I'd rather get on a plane
and travel to Paris or
disappear in Mexico
yet I sit here
in the garden growing old
I read *Mexico City Blues* a bit
perplexed, wondering
why the words we speak are made to bend
out of shape, why Jack Kerouac's
dour, why the people
who study writing generally read
more careful work, they see
professionalism as a goal
I see writing as a pool
of water rippling to the shore, I stand
by the water, it is cold, the colors collide
and become one conspiratorial force
that brings
a sense of mortality into focus
I see the sentimentality
buried in the poem, I feel the need to trim
Keroauc's prose, to forget the excess,
to embrace
a celebration of empty places, to kick a stone
across the pages, to retake the fortress
of a spooky death, his angel
brother, an early death, his own

in a barrage of alcohol, and
to be not quite so quick
to condemn anyone who ventures
onto the field, to see, even
those entrances
I might capture, to know

when it's good to lay down the pen
and to touch the fire
I'd rather open my notebook
to a rhododendron grove
where enemies live in the shadows I cast
on the dry, dusty ground it's so good
to be assessed by the silence,
it is okay to be told
what not to do by a god who walks
in brain, to trim the hedges
of my notebook
until the sun
is a copper penny, so fine
to let words lead the mind
as if they were amulets
forged by a shaman who believes
in the animal he wears on his head
I read Jack
way long ago, discombobulating trek

Érotique
portrait of PABLO PICASSO

Degas leans against a wall
dove, Cupid, flowers up his ass
India ink, wash, aquatint
Picasso is a bull in heat
the proprietress is an
amateur abortionist

the Pope takes a shit
Degas enjoys himself
in his portraits on
the whorehouse wall

handsome Raphael
dies in arms of Minotaur
Picasso ups the ante
with gouache, pastel, ink on paper
he is a wealthy combatant
in the eternal war

the terrace draws sea to it
everything is hidden
behind pastel walls
and an iron gate

the ball of fevered fire
Pablo in a stew
war time, cold winter
his pecker needed relief

Oh Francesco Goya
bring me the head
of Pablo Picasso

Stein Meditation
portrait of GERTRUDE STEIN

slow down
tie Paris to your crystal
animal

she controls a herd of paintings

her heart is a wishing well

Miss Stein was a barmaid in Carthage
she tiptoed into subversive libraries
and anointed unmarked sentences

take caution
today, this day
of invention

painted by Picasso
adored by Matisse

her atelier larger than
the universe

tears where toil trips
memory

bright funeral morning
flooding glass top

Seine flows
through your head
fate sees
those yellowed tops
of river barges
passing Notre Dame

Keep Me Simple
portrait of LANGSTON HUGHES

hearing nothing but the rivers
and those themes of deception
our dreams, bad boys
night restless we dream cards into
flesh, lash of the miracle, human
error, difficult to tear apart those heroes
of childhoods who oh who you . . .

your feelings run through my head
not words but feeling
not the heart of a poem
maker of the Weary Blues

here in 2015 the moon is a lunatic
you knew that already
poetry might understand

looming long Langston light troubles
for a stone road pick up a jawbone
throw no stone unless you are able
lonely man who wrote of Simple
I'll live to see men run to your song

Those Dark Trees
portrait of ROBERT FROST

poetic not pedantic
at moments delirious
curious and wry
surfacing on wicked plains
never young, haunted by
New England Autumn

old winter man
whose wishes were exposed
from the onset

he talked of gloom
of men facing the sea
of troubled roads
blueberries and
words wrenched
from desire

snow-white hair uncombed
facing a plate of words
to make of the experiment
something clear

all soon at noon
cramped room

beloved porcupine
of poetry
do you believe in justice?

you go down
yellow clouds pass
birches appear
go to town in horse and buggy

he made it through the inception
of aviation and beyond
his down-to-earth verse
blood memory he said

Frost proclaimed
poetry is power

she rises from twilight
has nowhere to go
but straight down the hall
and report to Dante

lullaby your death dream
light a muse for the candle

I want to walk by your side
great poet

'Poetry is the dawning of an idea'

I'd say choose your weapons
    and come out praising
    either hummingbird
  or butterfly or crusty
        farmers lugging baskets of apples
          toward town in a motor car

the poem is what a God is
if the God grows out of river mud

somehow you lived daylight
before we came round
and settled and lit bonfires
and boiled potatoes
while anointing bread
with marmalade

white sky lonesome deep and dark
you make a list of the poets
in *The Oxford Anthology*
of English Poetry

Maxwell of the Village
portrait of MAXWELL BODENHEIM

he never left
the streets of Greenwich Village
vending poems on street corners
when each neighborhood
held—oh Bohemia

dear Maxwell
please accept my joy
at your return
after decades of abuse

all those other poets
left you behind and then late in life
you wrote a book about the Village
and its character

you didn't not know Steve Dalachinsky
          or Irving Stettner

you wear ill-fitting suit
drinking yourself into a stupor
of boarded-up synagogues
and forgotten bars

I should have been a New York poet
of that golden generation
Alice Notley

Clark Coolidge
Anne Waldman
Bernadette Mayer
Ted Berrigan
Larry Fagin and Lewis Warsh

I might have been an angel of surprise
in my wild old man wintry
poet's disguise

Poe in the gutter
Whitman scrambles immortality
        at the end of his days

Maxwell, did you take a bath?
have you slept well
in a flimsy rented bed?
you made poetry simply night and day
as the muse requires

Two Things in One
portrait of EDNA ST. VINCENT MILLAY

"For what purpose, April, do you return again?"
Edna St. Vincent Millay
young vivacious poet star
moving to Greenwich Village, making a passageway
for light to walk through in graceful measure
you seem to have been slim and good-looking
you won the Pulitzer Prize at 23
because you wove baskets
because the written word floats
in a fast-flowing brook
you needed light of the earth
and an embrace from the sun

if I wrote your poems it wasn't intentional
I apologize from a new century in fact
it could be hubris and my desire
to cross-dress and transgress

how did you feel awakening
I am stalwart, devouring
the metaphors, preparing morning coffee
and beating eggs

Oh, Sailor
portrait of HART CRANE

where do you go?
from whose grasp are you fleeing?
why bother the ocean
when you could wreck a simple ditty
walking through the woods
of New York City?

I was 20, Hart,
when my poem for you was published
in a Florida magazine, "Epos"
a few people wrote
asking who I was because I sent you
tumbling to the bottom of the sea
off the ship

on that day of your wordless death
the rabbis stood in a circle
enchanted under shadows of the Brooklyn Bridge
they did not know your famous poem
in which the bridge serves us all

Hart Crane,
a sailor stares at you
you are excited
there is trouble

Hart will break your heart
you will go down

death has its own peculiar manner

take your upstate New York
difficult winter
you were barely
able to leave the house
take your improbable storm
on the Isle of Pines
I swear allegiance to pounding surf
of untouchable reverberation

Hart Crane, alone
wrenching words
resisting Longfellow
shaping elevators

trim those voyages
translucent magician
how you managed
to pry open ghost caravans
across what had been
rough land

Rimbaud 2023

I will try again
to reach the poet
from Charleville
even if my head
is filled with
roots of aging
redwood trees

I must find him
here in old age
no longer a long distance
seminarian of pagan
ritual

I have it on my mind
to unearth that sublime
adolescent poet
traipsing to Paris
through the silence
of Waterloo

on this occasion
ensconced in my studio
I live through the
Illuminations and his
Season in Hell

I find the man I wish I had been and the poet
I was never meant to be

I see Rimbaud
on a magic carpet
selling coffee beans
and other essentials
of the 19th century

I approach
nervously, unsure
prone to stumble

do I say Mr. Rainbow
or Arthur or honored
poet?

why don't I write
for the sea breeze
and a gull
flying across the rim
of time?

remember
Rimbaud obsessions
my art, I
want to
hug him and speak
perfect French
and steal him
from Paul Verlaine

“read to me
bad-ass poet
and let your dirty
mind sparkle
over the Arabian sand
put the bleached
remains of your song
into a deeper sound”

devour sleepy towns
in the French countryside
where the bourgeoisie
spoil everything
that blooms

I want to ask you
why you abandoned
the poem, but I am fearful
of what you’d say

let Verlaine go
to hell, I’m taking
charge of the
medieval turrets

I kiss your words
and jump over
your elegant
primeval dream
in which man is born
to properly bear silence
as he would
a storeroom, filled
with gold

At Ferlinghetti's Grave

do you watch him now
shadow bird
from Dylan Thomas's
death chant?

come to a party at
quiet Bolinas
covered in dust

do you see shadows
crossing the meridian
midafternoon?

say good morning
to eucalyptus
of the town cemetery

you never know
who is buried, I mean
you don't know
how someone is buried

do they keep counsel
on waves of earth?

if you ask the shadow bird
it will not make a difference

no you cannot run
and will not dream
beyond flight

what is it
that makes us
believe and bury
our dead?
the love
of shadows
ruins my sight

up into dead language
and dead ritual,
another poet
laid to rest
in catacombs of
elation and regret

78 Years

memories of the dilapidated
Greyhound bus station
limit the view

you'd go down there
like a conqueror
dreadlocks askew

the town was decaying
colorful strips of death abounded
wood finch and grackle sparred

the YMCA showed old comedies
boys with rotten teeth were around
to gather for a game in the tetherball yard

two days later in the Rocky Mountains
a blizzard tore off the face
of the President of the United States
coffee came in Styrofoam cups
the bogey man with a white beard
passed around a bottle of whiskey

you need to stand aside for the snowplows
they will do the job
and then the engines will turn
squirrels will dance design terrain

waitresses talk of bingo games
and capital punishment

60 years later I feel like an old man
listening to John Coltrane
on a cheap radio, somebody powerful
pours tequila over
concrete and cracked asphalt

tarantula and scorpion square off,
cold draft from the ample arms
of Walt Whitman, everything abuzz,
dreams died in the mud
and oil pool, love sucked into the tar

try to be an American Indian
on the far end of the Little Big Horn
try to be George Armstrong Custer
cut down by Crazy Horse just prior
to dropping bombs
on Hiroshima and Nagasaki

what if you were a 13-year-old boy
in the Buchenwald Death Camp?
What if a man in uniform
urinated on you
and then blew your brains out?

how fortunate I am
with an archive at
the Bancroft Library UC Berkeley,
books with my name on the cover
in many foreign tongues

I had no respect for those
who tortured the rose

there is no mountain
without a four-lane highway,
no life unless you appreciate
the perfume of dead pianists

I take a thermos of coffee on the bus
sandwich wrapped in cellophane
grope to my seat, gypsy princess decides
to stay behind giving extra room
as blinding snow hits
elk horns in a restless dream

the smoke of my own sanity
shaken by abuse, borne
over decades, hummingbird
twilights the garden on
the way to Xanadu

the last grizzly rambles down
from on high, we pull in late
to the depot, I am younger
than any old man
has the right to be

Lewis MacAdams
(1944–2020)

look really deep into what others may feel
drawn to the rivers as they flow through a mind
all praise to you, Lewis, who moved to L.A.
and cultivated shadows of the town, Yang-Na
before it became Our Lady, yes now, dear shade
I saw on the mesa, you were in a wheelchair
I found it impossible to take your hand,
you spoke of Joanne, outside I watched the trees
and spoke to Lorca, she smiled and hugged me

then you had gone away, there is a park
in Los Angeles, Lewis MacAdams Riverfront Park
for the living sounds you poured over
the concrete river, how like Williams you shared
a history, poet, activist, all honor to thru flow
of light, to the beds of water, to the labyrinthine
ideologues we all possess, yet you walked
"in thru shadow of the rose" to bring a wild music
back to life, quite some doing in sober drafts
of freeway ramps and metropolitan memory

I thank you for that river, for those particulars,
for your battle to reclaim the sun
and moon and river, to turn concrete
into grass to make us see, all praise then
to your quiet luminosity, one day walking
down by the river my father showed you

where he sat around a campfire, mid-Depression.
and you nodded and smiled, here's the twilight
of a dream, what is a river? oh well it might be
like poetry, maybe like a song nailed
onto the breeze of an emerging choir

My Sister's Spider

what do I know from the boughs
except that when the bough breaks
the cradle will rock

down come preconditions
set before me, so when I see
the spider turn on a window's edge
with a small house of webbing
enough time for dark and light
lunar and solar "things"
I bite into desire oh when the bough
breaks the cradle will rock
spider from this cell block
we awaken and walk
to the world's garden
sacrificing nothing
to the morning sun intruding
bathing this window in light
we believe this spider
has a sense of gratitude
even delight in rising
for the dawn we know
the spider holds both God
and Satan in esteem
for a moment anyway
it is my sister's spider
she puts out a dish of

spider food
empires rise
and fall
national flags
are torn to shreds
in the end
under the weight
of my sister's window

Aunt Bessie

when Aunt Bessie died we cordoned off
the Santa Monica Freeway
traffic ran slowly
down to the Los Angeles
International Airport
taxi drivers ranted
truckers gulped strong caffeine
we bought LSD
at the California Institute of Technology
from a grad student
who called himself Earth Pig
a girl named Nirvana Sunset
asked me to hop into bed
she did not understand
Vietnam as
condors soared
over the onramps

Aunt Bessie
forever chuckling
massive jowls moving
back and forth
a bowl of jelly

life continued—
we drove to the Memorial Park
digging a hole wide enough

Bessie fell
time to mourn
those babushkas
who came from Odessa
hoping to turn dust into gold

Mother Lived

when mother lived
rabbits covered her eyelids
with dust from a plough

she called on the air waves
to say she did not really expire
it was a clerical error
she would return in time

I've waited more than three decades
growing old and toothless
our house sold to a sheet metal worker
I made a fortune in 10-pound bond

Mother, remember your tambourine
and countless telephone marathons
making TV dinners, leaving
gardening to elderly Swedes

your father died in 1931
aggravating everyone
your high school friend Ramon
flew a biplane overhead

life is a mysterious pony
attended to by whispering angels
who made a congress out of poetry
and I said "Count me out"

I see you, yes I do
peeking at the chimney
in the house where we live

when the world died
we covered clouds
and shoveled dirt
into the pit

you owned a car
that said, "your blood
pressure is low"
hello!

the hand you offered
is a herd of bees
Sarah among the lions
in a land of ashen trees

you need only one life
one is plenty, we breathe
the breath of a gold god
who looks like me

you seem to be
a desert song east of Cairo
mother earth
father time

He Fought Aphids

portrait of SAM CHERRY

Sam rode a streak of lightning
across doomed earth
he wanted to play not pray
he loved silence not a series of demands
Sam of the spectral gods
my space
my din of night
the force field
handsome sam
and always wondering
how deep is far
and when do the animals
return?
sam loved the
quiet rumble
depression-era smoke
FDR and JFK goodbye hello
American anger
Sam in outer space,
time to do
everything
at once, to walk
in the fields
old Sam
dying man
hard-working sam
up and down

past the soviet flag
and the swarthy wolf
this is now
his time
he might be
growing younger
than the newly planted
corn

Fine Art of New York City

portrait of HERMAN CHERRY

I might enter the black cave
of Manhattan, slow walk
to buy cigars, passing remains
of Little Italy

where do you find
such divine talk?
we have Chinese
lunch underground
        yellow light

what a ritual to live and die
in a studio on Mercer Street
        surrounded by iron

may I presume
to offer innocence
in the antique afterglow
of lunch? Paint a tomb
for the unknown
lion tamer

such sacred time
Granny's son, father's
older brother
walrus mustache
curly hair, ideas

of torment
near-starvation
in Germany 1920
painting in a
cell of rats

as a kid, your mother
wore a red purse

        Herman, Herman . . .
what is love and
luck and who owns
the art? did you not
enjoy my imitation of
a young poet
sleeping with a beautiful
woman who designs
Broadway sets?

we drank
in your loft above
the diner
on Mercer Street
dressed in paintbrushes

your centrifuge in
bold joy

blue gash
yellow dab
red streak
orange cubes

why is dean untrained
subway car rambling?

I said goodbye
to the author
of Montauk
and of women
in a mirage
muscle-bound
New York City
in 1970
and gave myself
to Diana

later that night
on a bed of
pigments I fell
into a canvas
on your studio wall

how did you find
a third-floor hideout
where canvases are turned
towards the wall except for one
you named "cenotaph"
black block a patch of yellow

thinking back
from 2023
to the opening
of your show
oil on oil
the tint of late
antiquity

Self-Portrait in April

I feel like a
bamboo tree
in the national park
on one of those islands
or like a wolf
reinstated
in the wild

it is so easy
to brush it aside
and think only
of eroding hills
and of snow melt
come to tease men
into sublime
indifference

I am losing weight
and gaining wisdom
I am having ugly
dreams and beautiful
days, the aurora wails
across a serene
sense of old age

I talk to my father
nearly 20 years

dead, waiting for granny
at the seaside deli
where she counts
in Yiddish, so white
her hair like mine
today

I think of sweet
William, now an old
man, what would he say?
I tried to land
between his eyes
long ago

    oh and Diana
trading cigarettes
in our flat on
the Lower East Side

it's all we are
and will forever
be in the old
kingdom of
Tyrannosaurus rex

Neeli 1945–

Knee Lee Cherry
spelled NEELI CHERRY
son of Peter and Sally Rabbit
as white as newborn snow
until the world melts

in the beginning was a bird
and blocks of rock
and spewing fumes
and noxious odors
from prevailing gods
who have never died
though contemporary silence
spits in their eyes

so what if I am frantic
so what if I am mourning
the loss of one lover
or another
or that my little tree fort
sheltered me
back in 1963
already too old
for that sort of thing

I have a mother on
yellow wallflower paper

who sang of lambs and oats
and sent me to a changing
way beyond the clouds
because you see
in the beginning was the violence
Portrait of the Artist
as a Young Dog
Visions of Cody
The Picture of Dorian Gray
Pictures of the Gone World
Portrait of a Lady

in the beginning there
was everything
imaginable but not the word
creation is not perfect
the best minds of my generation
destroy themselves
teasing stupidity into existence

Neeli slept in the arms
of many slender warriors
and some bunny rabbits
and then he got old
he lost all his teeth
he talked about himself
as if the planet had been invented
for his own consumption

even this poem
is all about the dying rainforest
and a single frill plant
in plastic container

dying in the heat yesterday
till I gave her water
so that it may sing again

you tell me God is dead
the fuck, not by a long shot
it is men who die until nothing is left
but sunlight and shadow

in the beginning
was the ending
as late snow melted
carrying the demons
to the lowlands

if the gods are gone
how could you endure solitude?
there he goes again
talking about himself
a broken record in the hail

Yahweh

I don't want to waste your life
frying hamburger for an eternal lunch
pickles relish onion tomato
I'd rather make a BBQ
on one of the distant stars
and invite retired cops
to choose chicken or rib eye

I could make a burning bush
and part the Red Sea
and give Job a shellacking

my name is Yahweh
this is my self-portrait
I have a big white beard
and beautiful tan skin

if you think me ridiculous
just look in the mirror

I take everything personally
especially the bundled alfalfa
on both sides of the highway
from Milan to Parma

you killed me but I didn't die
you denied me but I came back
you shut the window
I entered through the door

"God is dead" you said
but then rotted
like an old tomato
and I lived on
skateboarding
in the clouds

I own a personal collection
of stars and star systems
and planets and black holes

I see what I do not see
I am what I am not I

if I am not God
what am I?
if I'm dead
what is light like
on the tip of a rusted nail
at the juncture
of good and evil?

what brutal falsehood
glitters like a diamond?

you will see me
in that light, the sparkle
that moves a man to tears

I never tell the truth
but I do show my wrath
and dive like Leviathan
into the starry blight

you disappear
with your hoard
of diamonds
in the portrait gallery
called existence

PHOTO BY KYLE HARVEY

NEELI CHERKOVSKI (July 1, 1945–March 19, 2024) was an American poet and memoirist. Born Nelson Cherry, he grew up in Los Angeles, where as a teen he began publishing poems and was befriended by Charles Bukowski, with whom he edited the poetry zine *Laugh Literary and Man the Humping Guns*. In the 1970s, he was a political consultant in the Riverside area, moving to San Francisco in 1974 to work for then-State Senator George Moscone. In San Francisco, he came out as gay, reclaimed his family's historical name, and became a major figure in the North Beach literary community. In the 1990s, he became a writer-in-residence at the New College of California, teaching literature and philosophy there until it closed in 2008.

The author of numerous collections of poetry, Cherkovski also wrote the first biographies of Lawrence Ferlinghetti (1979) and Charles Bukowski (1991), as well as *Whitman's Wild Children* (1988), a collection of his memoirs of 12 Beat Generation poets. He co-edited books, including *Anthology of L.A. Poets* (1972) and *The Collected Poems of Bob Kaufman* (2019). His collection *Leaning Against Time* won the 15th Annual PEN Oakland/Josephine Miles Literary Award in 2005. In 2017, he was awarded the Jack Mueller Poetry Prize by Lithic Press, which published his 400-page, career-spanning *Selected Poems 1959–2022* in 2024. Cherkovski is also the subject of the documentary film *It's Nice to Be with You Always* (2020). He lived in San Francisco with Jesse Cabrera, his partner of 40 years.

Neeli Cherkovski's papers are housed at the Bancroft Library, University of California, Berkeley.

It's Nice to Be with You Always can be seen here: https://www.youtube.com/watch?v=RNjCh-6GoLo

PHOTO OF NEELI CHERKOVSKI AND LAWRENCE FERLINGHETTI BY IRA NOWINSKI

Books by Neeli Cherkovski

Poems for the Wailing Wall (Black Cat Press, 1968)
Pre-Rabbinic Poems (Tecumseh Press, 1969)
Don't Make a Move (Tecumseh Press, 1973)
The Waters Reborn (Red Hill Press, 1975)
Public Notice (Beatitude, 1975)
Ferlinghetti, A Biography (DoubleDay, 1979)
Love Proof (Green Light Press, 1980)
Home American: Section 1 (Deep Forest, 1983)
Juggler Within (Harwood Alley Monographs, 1983)
Clear Wind (Avant Books, 1984)
Whitman's Wild Children (Lapis Press, 1988)
Hank: The Life of Charles Bukowski (Random House, 1991)
Animal (Pantograph Press, 1996)
Elegy for Bob Kaufman (Sun Dog Press, 1996)
Leaning Against Time (R.L. Crow Publications, 2004)
Naming the Nameless (Sore Dove Press, 2004)
Einstein Alive (Solo Zone, 2005)
From the Canyon Outward (R.L. Crow Publications, 2009)]
From the Middle Woods (New Native Press, 2011)
Manila Poems (Bottle of Smoke Press, 2013)
Elegy for My Beat Generation (Lithic Press, 2018)
In the Odes (Magra Books, 2018)
Coolidge & Cherkovski: In Conversation (Lithic Press, 2020)
Hang on to the Yangtze River (Lithic Press, 2020)
Bukowski, A Life (Black Sparrow Press, 2020)
ABCs (Spuyten Duyvil, 2021)
Ferlinghetti, A Life (Black Sparrow Press, 2022)
Selected Poems 1959–2022 (Lithic Press, 2024)
The Portrait Gallery Called Existence (City Lights Books, 2025)